MENTOR FIELD GUIDE

REWRITING THE FATHERLESS STORY THROUGH MENTORING

THE MENTORING PROJECT

Copyright © 2014 by The Mentoring Project

All rights reserved. No portion or excerpt of this publication may be reproduced, copied, distributed, projected, stored in a retrieval system, displayed or transmitted in any form or by any means whether electronic, mechanical, photocopy, recording, scanning, projection or other medium now known or later created, except for brief quotations as included in critical reviews, scholarly presentations or articles, without the prior express written permission of John Sowers via The Mentoring Project, Inc. Any brief quotations used in critical reviews, scholarly presentations or articles must be expressly credited to this publication by page number and to The Mentoring Project, Inc.

To request usage permission regarding this publication, please contact advocate@thementoringproject.org

THE MENTORING PROJECT, TMProject and @TMPROJECT are trademarks held and protected by The Mentoring Project, Inc.

CONTENTS

★ ★ ★ ★ ★ ★

Recommendations for The Mentoring Project's Mentor Field Guide

"I'm grateful for the work of John Sowers and The Mentoring Project. They are doing amazing work to ensure young people are loved, challenged and given second chances."

Jeremy Courtney, Founder/Author of Preemptive Love: Pursuing Peace One Heart at a Time

"The Mentoring Project is the front runner on equipping the church how to mentor fatherless children. Their training material is simple to use and highly effective! At Generation Outdoors we use the TMP training material to equip all our mentors."

John Church, Co-Founder Generation Outdoors, Austin, Texas

"We have been mentoring at-risk and gang involved youth in Chicago for the last 6 years and have used The Mentoring Project's mentor training materials to train our team for the last few years. This has been a great resource in training new mentors and we are excited to continue to use it going forward! I highly recommend this for any church wanting to mentor young people in their city!

Pastor Matt DeMateo.
New Live Community Church, Chicago, Illinois

JOHN SOWERS

PRESIDENT

John Sowers became President of The Mentoring Project in 2009 after serving the Billy Graham Association as a multi-language coordinator. He is the author of *Fatherless Generation: Redeeming the Story* (October 2010) and *The Heroic Path* (May 2014). In 2012, John was honored at the White House as one of President Obama's Champions of Change in the area of fatherhood and healthy families. As a mentor advocate, he spends time consulting schools, businesses, mentor organizations and conducting large mentor training events. John works with the White House and the U.S. Department of Justice on their yearly Fatherhood Initiative. His work has been featured on CNN, Fox News, Christianity Today and RELEVANT magazine. He speaks at gatherings such as The Justice Conference, Q Ideas, Story Chicago, CAFO Orphan Summit, Verge, Idea Camp, Long Live Mentoring and others. John completed his M.DIV at Trinity Theological Seminary and his D.MIN at Gordon Conwell.

DONALD MILLER

FOUNDER//SPOKESPERSON

Author Donald Miller founded The Mentoring Project in 2008. Don continues to be involved with The Mentoring Project by advocating for mentors and for the fatherless. Don serves as the spokesperson for The Mentoring Project and champions our annual "Don't Buy the Tie" campaign that launches each year around Father's Day. The Mentoring Project uses Don's books to inspire and equip mentors.

FOREWORD

Dear Friend,

We're thrilled you are willing to serve your community by attending a mentor training using The Mentoring Project's training resources. We exist to equip you to rewrite the fatherless story through mentoring. We recruit and train mentors to show up for at-risk and high-risk youth and fatherless children. Our goal is for you to establish a sustainable mentoring community in your own context that is the foundation for long-term, transformative relationships.

On the local level, The Mentoring Project functions as a community-based mentoring program, serving with partner sites where we recruit, train, and match mentors. These sites inform our global mentor training experiences. We capture our training best practices in book / video format for you to use in your own context. It is our goal to provide you with the very best faith-based training materials. These training resources are used in over 300 cities and eight countries.

MENTOR FIELD GUIDE

The Mentor Field Guide was designed to be a pocket reference for you to help with your mentoring relationship. These mentoring principles can be broadly applied, used with a parenting relationship, with a community-based mentor match, or even with friends. I believe we are all

mentoring someone, whether we realize it or not.
The main objectives of this Field Guide are to:

1. **Establish your commitment to be a mentor**

2. **Provide tools to equip and sustain you as a mentor**

The Mentor Field Guide outlines how to engage by building trust and how to be effective as a mentor. It is our hope that you leave the training confident and ready to begin your mentoring relationship. This training is a critical first step in preparing you for the realities of mentoring.

Please understand the training is not the final piece of becoming a mentor – rather, it is an introduction. Follow us on Twitter - @TMProject – and sign up for our **Mentor Collective (https://tmp.webconnex.com/mentorcollective)**, to receive mentor resources and encouragement on a regular basis. Thank you!

The best is yet to be,

Dr. John Sowers
President, The Mentoring Project
@johnsowers

Fatherlessness is a personal tragedy and a collective epidemic. Some 25 million American kids are growing up without dad. One third of those will never see their fathers. Fatherlessness is the engine driving some of our worst social problems, from gangs and youth violence, to teenage pregnancy, drug abuse, school dropouts and suicide. Mentoring intersects this sad trajectory and allows a child to hope for a better future. Mentoring is the method to rewrite the fatherless story.

John Sowers, President, The Mentoring Project

I believe in the power of story and invite you into the new story we are telling. I believe we can rewrite the fatherless story. This narrative does not have to be cyclical. It can end with fewer men in prisons, less families abandoned, and the fatherless being cared for by positive role models who believe, like I do, that we can choose to live a better story.

Donald Miller, Founder, The Mentoring Project

BACKGROUND OF MENTORING

PART ONE

1

Rewriting the Fatherless Story
Chapter One

Fatherlessness has become a defining feature of American childhood.

In many neighborhoods, children with fathers are now the exception to the rule. Millions of fathers are leaving (and have left) their wives, girlfriends and children to find better fortunes somewhere else, somewhere on the greener side of the fence. This is a newer social phenomenon and we are just beginning to see the effects.

In the United States, some 20 million children are growing up in single parent homes, searching for dad. But dad is nowhere to be found. He left when he got his girlfriend pregnant and will never see his child. Or he ran off to another city, to start another franchise family. Or he is incarcerated – locked away. Or he is home, but lost in substance abuse, alcoholism, for some reason unable to engage. Rejection is the defining feature of the fatherless generation.

The epidemic of fatherlessness is heartbreaking – but even more, it is destructive.

Numerous studies have shown that fatherlessness is the engine driving our most urgent social problems. Fatherlessness is the elephant in the room – in every room. According to the studies, children from fatherless homes account for some:

- 63% of youth suicides
- 71% of pregnant teenagers

- 70% of youth in state-operated institutions
- 80% of rapists motivated with displaced anger
- 85% of youth who exhibit behavior disorders
- 90% of homeless and runaway children

Even more, children from fatherless homes are nearly twice as likely to struggle with hyperactivity, conduct and emotional disorders and have a social impairment. Three times as likely to be struggling in school or have repeated a grade. Five times more likely to be poor. Thirty-three times more likely to be seriously abused. Seventy-three times more likely to be killed.[1]

We see fatherlessness in a school we visit in Florida, with ninety teenage pregnant moms. We see fatherlessness in the gang-related shootings of Chicago, over five hundred shootings in 2013. We see fatherlessness in the face of children who hurt and abuse themselves. Author David Blankenhorn writes:

"Fatherlessness is the most harmful demographic trend of this generation. It is the leading cause of declining child well-being in our society. Yet, despite its scale and social consequences, fatherlessness is a problem that is frequently ignored or denied."

This fatherless story is seen in every neighborhood. In every city we work with or consult, there is a waiting list for mentors. These waiting lists are full of fatherless children who have been signed up by their mom. Now they are waiting for a mentor. Many of these children will never be matched with one.

We receive countless emails and phone calls from single moms and people of all ages who are dealing with a father-absence wound. We recently received this letter from Chris:

1 Excerpt from Fatherless Generation: Redeeming the Story, by John Sowers, HarperCollins Publishing, New York, NY, 2010, pp. 35-36

Coming from a home where I didn't have a father was really hard on me. My mother did her best but worked a ton of hours as a correction officer. I am now thirty years old and unable to hold down a relationship or a job.

I never had a father figure. My mom's husband threatened me with violence and called me awful names. After reading Fatherless Generation, I realized I wasn't the only one. I've had anger issues my whole life, constantly getting into fights and exploding. I met my father two years ago. It didn't turn out well – and I wound up fathering him and babying his guilt for not being around. Thank you for hearing my story – and thank you for all you do!

This generation has been wounded most in relationship and it is in relationship where healing must begin. This is our driving mission: to heal a wounded generation through relationship. We don't put energy into blaming fathers or mothers. We cheer single moms and dads who are trying the best they can. There are millions of single, heroic moms who are raising children well. There are also tons of divorced fathers who are very involved with their children.

At The Mentoring Project, we are laser-focused on empowering people – like you – to rewrite the fatherless story through mentoring. There are millions of children all around us who need help, right now. Every day we have the privilege to see mentors step up as the quiet heroes of the movement.

Every child needs a father.
But not every child has one.
This is where a mentor steps in.

Mentors drastically shaped my life.

When I was five, Tom showed up at my door. My brother and I lived with my mom, as my dad had left us three years earlier – moved to a different state. After that, we saw him once a year. Dad was elusive and became a faceless voice on the phone, a signature on a birthday card, an old yellow Polaroid picture.

Needless to say, men were a rare if not extinct species in my life.

Tom had a crooked smile and black hair slicked over to the side, and to my six-year old eyes, he was really, really hairy. The first time we hung out together, Tom took me to the Baskin-Robbins ice cream shop. At first, I wasn't sure what to think about him, but he dispelled my worries when he bought me two scoops of chocolate ice cream. As we drove home in his little blue pickup truck, he told me there was a ghost on the roof. We both screamed in terror-filled delight.

I was sold.

Tom and I continued to hang out a few times a month. Later, we went fishing together at Lake Maumelle, stopping at a place called the Jolly Roger Marina. The Jolly Roger was pirate-themed, with a black skull-and-crossbones flag flying outside the door. Upon entering the Jolly Roger, we met a crusty man named Ol' Verl who rented us a boat. Our simple fishing trip was turned into a wild, pirate adventure, and we talked about Ol' Verl for years after.

For the rest of the day, Tom and I adopted pirate accents and said "Argh" a lot. We rented a little green boat from Ol' Verl and set out for the lake deep seas. At the end of the day, we had only managed a few small bass – but it didn't matter to me. I was loving life with my new pirate-mentor Tom.

I knew our time was short, so I kept asking him for "one more cast." I'll never forget my last cast of the day, when I landed a largemouth bass – and Tom went nuts. He made me feel like I had just won American Idol, cheering and clapping and screaming.

THE MENTORING PROJECT

EVERY CHILD NEEDS A FATHER. BUT NOT EVERY CHILD HAS ONE. THIS IS WHERE A MENTOR STEPS IN.

@JOHNSOWERS | @TMPROJECT

#MENTOR

This was a life-anchoring moment.

A few years later, Tom was called into ministry and moved to Dallas. After he moved, I was matched with another mentor, Sonny.

Sonny grew up in rural Arkansas, hunting and fishing, and he worked for one of the state utility companies. Sonny and I spent a lot of time in the woods, tracking deer and other critters. He taught me how to still-hunt, walk like a ghost, cut sign, and move impossibly slow.

Every night before our hunt, Sonny would unroll a topographical map and notice the valleys and hills and ditches and water sources. He could tell by looking at that map where the bucks would move and where the general deer population was moving. In the dozens of times I hunted with him, he was never wrong.

He bought me a rifle when I was eight years old, and that fall I took my first buck. I was hooked. I fell in love with the woods. I've been a tracker ever since.

Later, Sonny and I were wrestling – real wrestling – flying feet, smashing things. Sonny was tossing me around like a leaf. He was being rough, but careful not to hurt me. But to the untrained eye, I'm sure it seemed too rough. His wife, Cindy, was there and she said, "Be careful, Sonny, don't hurt him."

Sonny replied, "Are you kidding me? This boy is tougher than an oak knot."

The first time anyone called me tough. It was over twenty years ago, but I remember it like it was yesterday. It's the first time a man called me tough or strong. I think every boy needs to hear that. Every boy needs to know he has resilience and can fight through things, even things he cannot win. Years later, Sonny came and stood on the sidelines of my high school football games and cheered for me as I played safety and tackled guys.

Tom and Sonny taught me things about being a man – Tom helped me laugh and gave me permission to use my imagination. He was the first guy to help me understand that manhood was approachable. If being a man was being like Tom, I liked that vision of manhood – and I could be that.

Sonny helped me overcome things. Things like the woods. Hunting. Tracking. He was more serious than Tom, but he helped me find and do things that I still love today. He taught me resilience – toughness – being strong like a tree in the face of adversity.

Both men sacrificed their time and life to be mentors and father figures in my life. Because of their sacrifice, I learned that being a man was not nearly as intimidating as I made it out to be. I didn't have to be afraid of men – or afraid of becoming one myself.[2]

Finding a mentor for every child who needs one is our mandate.

Recruiting and training mentors is our mission.

We believe you can make a difference.

2 Excerpt taken from Fatherless Generation: Redeeming the Story, by John Sowers, Zondervan, Grand Rapids, Michigan, 2010, pp. 89-92.

For a more in-depth overview of the fatherless crisis, please read: *Fatherless Generation: Redeeming the Story*, by The Mentoring Project President, Dr. John Sowers.

2

A MENTOR IS A TRUSTED FRIEND.

@JOHNSOWERS | @TMPROJECT

#MENTOR

A Mentor Defined
Chapter Two

A mentor is a trusted friend.

Whether we realize it or not, we are all mentoring someone. We are all modeling something; our lives tell a story. We are all influencing someone. At The Mentoring Project, we train and equip mentors so they are focused and intentional. There are several types of mentors:

One type is the **professional mentor**, where the mentoring relationship is based on vocational / career goals. This mentoring takes place between two working adults, and the focus is usually content aimed at helping another person succeed and advance at work. Usually one person is the guru and one person is the apprentice, and the focus is transmitting information from guru to apprentice and setting goals. Often this commitment is only for a set amount of time. The aim of this type of mentoring is not personal relationship but information, career advancement and accomplishments.

Another type is the **spiritual mentor**. Similar to the professional mentor, this type of relationship is often content focused. In many circles this is called a discipleship relationship – and there are pre-set goals and agreements about what books to read, Bible verses to memorize and other spiritual goals. Also, in this type of mentoring both people usually share the same spiritual worldview, and this worldview and the presuppositions are agreed upon before meeting.

Programmatic excellence, training, sustainability – these are critical. In any program, the safety of the child is always first. Always. We believe the programs are "rails" for the relationship. The program is not the end, but the means. The relationship is the goal. If we are only checking off boxes for a program, then we make little impact. But if we are involved and trusted relationally, we can change the trajectory of a child.

Mentors cannot fully replace an absent father. But mentors can accomplish a great deal – through consistent, loving presence. Mentoring is not a "quick fix," because building relationships is slow, and results can take years and be hard to measure. In 2013, The Center for Addiction and Mental health released the results of a five-year, 1000 participant mentee study. This study found that:

- Students with a mentor are significantly more confident in their academic abilities and considerably less likely to display behavior problems.
- Girls with a mentor are four times less likely to fight, lie, bully or express anger than girls without a mentor.
- The positive effects of mentoring apply to students regardless of the child's age, personal history, family circumstance or cultural identity.
- Girls with a mentor are two and a half times more likely to be confident in their ability at school.
- Boys with a mentor are three times less likely to suffer from peer-pressure anxiety or worrying about what other children say about them.
- Boys with a mentor are two times more likely to do well in school.
- Boys with a mentor are two times less likely to develop negative conduct like bullying, fighting, lying, cheating, losing their temper or expressing anger.

Mentoring works.

At The Mentoring Project, we are privileged to see these tiny stories unfold every day. Stories like Quinn and Xavier, who spend time together once a week. Here is a snippet of their story:

> Once homework is done – hoops for dessert. Quinn helps Xavier shoot a free-throw. During rest breaks, Xavier secretly tells us that he looks forward to Quinn's visits so he can beat him at one-on-one. They both laugh. Quinn is the one man who believes in Xavier and shows up for him. Xavier says, 'I like hanging out with Quinn, and he is gonna be a great dad someday. I wish he were mine.'

Thousands of boys are growing up without a dad. In some urban settings, the number of single-parent households is close to 70%. What if thousands of people – like you – stepped up and showed up for this generation as mentors?

What if there was a mentor for every child in need?

How would that change a generation?

How would it change you?

3

THE MENTORING PROJECT

CARING FOR THE FATHERLESS IS CENTRAL TO GOD'S HEART AND MUST BE CENTRAL TO OUR HEARTS AS WELL.

@JOHNSOWERS | @TMPROJECT

#MENTOR

God's Heart for the Fatherless Chapter Three

> *"Father to the fatherless, a defender of widows is God in his holy dwelling." – Psalm 68.5*

With all of the cause-driven activity today, the issue of fatherlessness is easily lost in the frenzy. But according to James 1.27, reaching the fatherless is not an optional act of benevolence. James writes, "True religion our Father accepts is to care for the widows and orphans in their distress."

According to James, how we respond (or do not respond) to the fatherless is a measure of the integrity of our faith. Fatherlessness is not just another cause, another cause booth in the science-fair of cause. It is a critical measure of our faith. This eliminates our options; if we are people of faith, we must be involved in reaching the fatherless.

Caring for the fatherless is central to God's heart and must be central to our heart as well.

God identifies Himself with the fatherless – and even takes it as one of His names, Father to the fatherless. If our God is Father to the fatherless, how can we, who are called to be imitators of Him, be any less?

He names Himself: Father, Protector, Defender and Provider for the fatherless. These themes are woven throughout scripture. Psalm 146.9 says, "God watches over the alien and sustains the fatherless and the widow." Hosea 14.3 says, "In you the fatherless find compassion."

In another example, Job loses everything. His land. His family. His health. And after he was mocked by his wife and friends, they began to question his integrity. Some of their accusations centered on Job's treatment of the poor and the least of these. His "friends" accused him of neglecting the fatherless, to which Job replied,

> Whoever heard me spoke well of me, because I rescued the poor and cried for help, and the fatherless who had no one to assist him. If I kept bread to myself, not sharing with the fatherless, if I have raised my hand against the fatherless, then let my arm fall from my shoulder, let it be broken off at the joint. (Job 29.11, 31.17, 21-22)

The biblical mandate is clear – **God measures the integrity of our faith by how we respond to the fatherless.** The question is not if we will engage the fatherless, but how we will engage. God's heart for the fatherless and mandate to look after them should compel us to ask:

How do I get involved with this issue? Do I look after the needs of the fatherless? Do I pray for the fatherless, give money to help, and mentor them? Is protecting, providing, defending and fathering the fatherless a part of my faith?

Mentoring is a great place to start.

THE MENTORING PROJECT

GOD MEASURES THE INTEGRITY OF OUR FAITH BY HOW WE RESPOND TO THE FATHERLESS.

@JOHNSOWERS | @TMPROJECT

#MENTOR

4

"GOD IS MOVING THROUGH PEOPLE AND THROUGH ONE-ON-ONE RELATIONSHIPS TO ACCOMPLISH GREAT THINGS."

-REV. BILLY GRAHAM

#MENTOR

Mentoring as The Way Forward Chapter Four

In his book, *The Next Christians*, Gabe Lyons discusses a personal conversation he had with evangelist and statesman Billy Graham. The two met in Graham's home and shared cookies together. After sharing for thirty minutes, Graham reflected:

> Back when we did these big crusades in football stadiums and arenas, the Holy Spirit was really moving – and people were coming to Christ as we preached the Word of God. But today, I sense something different is happening. I see evidence that the Holy Spirit is working in a new way. **God is moving through people and through one-on-one relationships to accomplish great things.** People are demonstrating God's love to those around them, not just with words, but in deed.[3]

Graham was reflecting on something critical for us to understand. American culture has changed. The world has changed. Ways to reach people have also changed. Fifty years ago, even twenty-five years ago, people were willing to come to a crusade, a church service or a religious meeting. This is not the case today. People still come to religious meetings and church services, but the broad, cultural expectation of "going to church" has died.

We need to change our strategic thinking. It is no longer enough to just invite people into what we are doing. It is no longer enough to make a slick church service and cross our fingers and hope they come to our building. They are not coming.

3 Excerpt from: The Next Christians, Seven Ways You Can Live the Gospel and Restore the World, by Gabe Lyons, Multnomah Books, Portland, Oregon, 2012, pp. 15-16.

Instead of inviting people into consuming another religious service, we need to “Go” as we are called in Matthew 28, and become missional, incarnational, and relational. Service projects and community events are good things and they open the door for future relationships,but they are not relational mentoring. It is easier to mobilize 1000 people to rake leaves once a year than it is to have 10 committed people be available once a week to mentor a child. We must open our eyes wide to the people around us and then walk to and with them.

This is the story of the Good Samaritan.

> A man was going down from Jerusalem to Jericho, when he was attacked by robbers. They stripped him of his clothes, beat him and went away, leaving him half dead. A priest happened to be going down the same road, and when he saw the man, he passed by on the other side. So too, a Levite, when he came to the place and saw him, passed by on the other side. But a Samaritan, as he traveled, came where the man was; and when he saw him, he took pity on him. He went to him and bandaged his wounds, pouring on oil and wine. Then he put the man on his own donkey, brought him to an inn and took care of him. The next day he took out two coins and gave them to the innkeeper. ‘Look after him,’ he said, ‘and when I return, I will reimburse you for any extra expense you may have.’ ‘Which of these three do you think was a neighbor to the man who fell into the hands of robbers?’ (Luke 10.30-36)

A man is mugged, stripped and left for dead. Two religious men see him, a Priest and a Levite, but walk by him, passing for another more pressing need. In my mind, I see these two crossing to the other side of the road to avoid the fallen man, or walking and stepping over him. It is curious that Jesus would identify these men as religious leaders. These religious men quite possibly would be headed to the synagogue, to church, as was their daily custom. In this sense, these men might have been “stepping over” the fallen man because they were on a more urgent, religious mission.

Another man, not one identified with religion, a Samaritan, sees the fallen man, stops and helps him. It is curious why Jesus identifies the "half-breed," as the other two men were obviously religious. The Samaritan was not identified with religion, and there was some racism directed towards Samaritans.

When Jesus asks, *"Which of these loves his neighbor?"* the answer is obvious. It is not the religious men who step over him in the name of religion. It is the one who *stops and helps.*

This is our call. To stop and help. This is how we love our neighbor. This is how we love and reach a generation.

According to Jesus, we cannot step over the fatherless child and the single mom and still love our neighbor. We cannot go to church and leave them stranded on the road. We are not fulfilling the Greatest Commandment if we step over them in the name of religion. Our call is to stop and help.

Fatherless youth and single moms are the most reachable unreached people group.

This is our mission. It is a relational one. This is relational theology. The Samaritan's call to love our neighbor is a relational one. The Greatest Commandment is relational. The Great Commission is 100% relational. Reaching the fatherless and the widow is 100% relational.

We either love our neighbor in relationship or we do not.

We also miss this goal as long as we believe mission is somewhere out there far away. But the scales of justice are balanced. The international orphan and the fatherless child right in front of us are equal. They are both neighbors. Unless we have a clear, specific call, we cannot step over the one in front of us to go to the one far away.

This is the call of the early believers in Acts 1:8. "You will be my witnesses in Jerusalem, Judea, Samaria and to the ends of the earth."

First here.
Then across the tracks.
Then the next town over.
Then the rest of the world.

For some reason, we default to the last – "to the ends of the earth." Or else we think that the last is somehow more spiritual. But unless we are witnesses "here – right here" we don't have the right to choose the last one.

At-risk and high risk youth are here. In your neighborhood. On the soccer team with your child. At your school. In your church. Perhaps even next door. Here.

Mentoring is manifestation of the one-on-one relationships Billy Graham talked about. This is relational theology. We must get up close to our neighbor. To love our neighbor, we must stop and help those in need. This world will never believe our gospel – that God can be their Father – until we are willing to step into their lives with the same intimacy that Jesus entered into ours at the Incarnation. This is our way forward.

FATHERLESS YOUTH AND SINGLE MOMS ARE THE MOST REACHABLE UNREACHED PEOPLE GROUP.

@JOHNSOWERS | @TMPROJECT

#MENTOR

5

Reverse Mentoring Chapter Five

It is easy to think of mentoring as "us helping them," as a "top-down model" when in reality it is really us helping each other, as a "side by side" model. Make no mistake, the adult is the responsible one and the one who dictates much of the process. The adult initiates and plans and shows up at school or in the community and asks deeper questions and coaches when appropriate. To think of mentoring only as a "top-down" model is incomplete and far from true. Mentoring is a mutually-beneficial relationship.

Recently, I watched Josh DuBois, the former White House Director of Faith Based Initiatives and Neighborhood Partnerships, share his mentoring story about meeting his mentee, Aidid. When he met Aidid, Josh was at Boston University and had a strong drive to make a mark in politics. Josh was smart, finishing Cum Laude, and driven, refusing to take no for an answer when he was interviewing with a local politician. Josh said,

> When I started mentoring Aidid – my vision began to change. I started seeing other people and their needs and desires. Because of my own personal determination to make a difference, I didn't see other people and their perspectives well. Aidid changed that.

Mentoring blesses everyone involved.

This is the great joy and surprise of mentoring, when we discover Jesus' words to be true, "It is better to give than to receive." (Acts 20.35) As we find the courage to step forward and give our lives away for the sake of another, we find fulfillment greater than anything we could ever receive.

In the business world, this idea of "Reverse Mentoring" was popularized by former GE Chairman, Jack Welsh. It is where the older leaders of an organization open themselves to the younger, rising leaders and learn from them. Younger leaders have fresh eyes, creative ideas and new worldview, dreams and visions.

In a youth-mentoring context, "Reverse Mentoring" simply means being open to observe, listen and learn from both parties. It takes humility, especially on the mentor's part, to create space and genuinely learn from a mentee. Some lead from a "platform" – above, and others lead from the "street" – beside.

Mentoring is leading from the side.

I believe the next generation of leaders will lead from the street, from beside.

This idea is being played out in our country nearly every day. Recently, we saw a police officer, Captain Johnson, step into the streets of Ferguson and walk beside the protestors. Within 24 hours after he took over, all of the tear gas stopped – it was traded in for hugs. Captain Johnson marched with protestors, protecting their (peaceful) right to protest. He had all the police officers take off their gas masks and SWAT gear. He calmed the whole thing down. He was leading from the street.

During the same week of his incarnational servant-leadership, there were several high-profile leadership conferences happening. I thought the contrast was interesting. There were dozens of leaders speaking about leadership – including me. Certainly, many of these leaders speaking from the platform also lead beside, and for many of them, this is how they earned the right to be heard.

But there were a few other speakers who are primarily "bullhorn" leaders who speak loudly at audiences from their platform. While their content is valuable, I think those who quietly walk beside, like Captain Johnson, are

THE MENTORING PROJECT

MENTORING IS LEADING FROM THE SIDE.

@JOHNSOWERS | @TMPROJECT

#MENTOR

louder. Even more, I believe that the future of leadership in our country belongs to the quiet leaders who influence thousands of people, one at a time, even if they never speak at a leadership conference or write a book and remain in relative or complete anonymity.

My first mentor, Tom, led this way.

He was consistently in my life for several years until he moved away to another state. We kept in touch for years, as Tom sent cards and called. Even those distant relational touches were important.

Eventually, when I graduated high school and went to college, Tom and I lost touch. Several years later, I found the church where he pastored and sent him an email. I thanked him for being a great mentor and told him I had written about him in *Fatherless Generation*. This is what Tom wrote in his reply,

> I remember Ol' Verl! One of my favorite things I have done with my boys is introduce them to colorful people like Verl along the way. And I still have the picture frame that holds three small pictures of you holding up the two perch you caught.
>
> Also, I wasn't the primary reason we got along; it was you. You were the perfect "Little Brother." I had no idea what I was doing. I simply thought I could help. Had you not been so welcoming and open and eager and smiling and obviously bright and brave, it never would have worked. So thank you! I hope you give yourself credit.

TOOLS FOR THE MENTOR

PART TWO

6

Tools: Overview
Chapter Six

This section lays the foundation for your mentoring relationship. Rather than overwhelm you with information, we have narrowed down the Mentor Tools into three foundational relational principles.

These principles are necessary for building trust and forming a long-term sustainable relationship. Our goal is trust-building. See each of these tools as steps, as building blocks for trust in your relationship. Trust is the bedrock of your mentoring relationship. You will see this focus on relationship as a repeated theme over and over again. This is because mentoring works best when it is not seen as a program or a "time slot" but as a caring friendship with the potential to last for years. Building and keeping trust is the bedrock of your mentoring relationship.

Your mentee will not let down his guard until trust is established. It may well take longer to establish trust in this situation. If your mentee is from a single-parent, high-risk or fatherless home, he or she may have a deep mistrust of authority. Your mentee may even "test" your authority as a proxy for testing your commitment. He may wonder, "Will this person leave me too, like everyone else has?"

The tools listed in this section are in sequential order, with building trust in mind. The first way we build trust is by "showing up." Then after initial trust is established, we continue to build trust by modeling good character, by "living out." Finally, after trust is established by our presence and by modeling, we earn the right to be heard. We "coach" or speak into a mentee's life with grace and truth. Regardless of the mentor tool for which you are applying, we lead with love, and like I Timothy 1:5, "The goal of our instruction is love."

These tools are useful for building relationship, and they are also vital for our ongoing relationship. We never "graduate" from these tools – they are our standing marching orders. These tools stay with us for the rest of our lives and inform all of our relationships, for deepening trust.

Also, these tools are measuring sticks for the mentor. Use these tools to evaluate success. Mentors sometimes get burned out and quit when they're not sure they are making a difference. When you think or feel this way, come back. Review these tools, and keep them in the forefront of your mind.

Remember that your success is measured on your faithfulness. *Show up* faithfully, *live out* humility and integrity, and *speak in* with grace and truth. If you are doing these things consistently, even if your mentee is not responding quickly, you are being faithful. If you do these things, your impact may not be immediately felt or measurable, but you are making a profound, unspoken difference. It may not be visible for years, and you may never realize the impact you are having on that child, how much he or she looks up to you, talks about you, thinks about you. You are making a difference.

7

THE MENTORING PROJECT

MENTORS WIN BY SHOWING UP.

@JOHNSOWERS | @TMPROJECT

#MENTOR

Tool One: Show Up
Chapter Seven

Mentors win by showing up.

The first and most important thing a mentor brings is presence. Your unconditional presence is the anchor of the mentoring relationship. This foundation is formed over time, and it builds trust as a child learns that you are there.

Showing up is 90% of your mentoring relationship. The great thing about showing up is that anyone can do it. You don't have to be rich or famous or smart or cool or trendy, or any of those things – you just have to be available. This is the best gift we can offer a child: unconditional and faithful presence. This is your foundation. If the mentor is not faithfully present, the relationship will not grow.

Fatherlessness brands a generation with rejection; presence embraces a generation with acceptance.

Presence is the opposite of what many children experience. It is not uncommon for fatherless children to see a "revolving door" of authority figures in their lives. Even if mom is around consistently, she may work three jobs, be in school, and carry all of the other burdens of the household. Also, male authority figures may be non-existent, making them impossible to "count on" and trust. Presence helps re-establish trust.

Those who mean the most to us are those who show up in our lives.

I was blessed to have many people show up for me. My mom worked three jobs so she was intentional about finding mentors for me - Tom and Sonny and others. My mom was very supportive as was my grandmother.

> "My grandmother moved from the country to the city to help raise us while Mom worked. She picked me up from school every afternoon, getting there an hour early to make sure she was first in line. She drove me home and stayed with me until Mom arrived, usually around five or six.
>
> She taught me things. How to draw straight lines. Write cursive. Love books. In the summers, she took me to art classes and the library. We always did the summer reading program together. I got lost under piles of old dusty books. The library is still my favorite place, it reminds me of her.
>
> When I left for college, Grandmother sent me a hand-written card every week. She always used a Monet print and filled the card with words, saying she loved me, was proud of me, and was praying for me. She sent her cards every week, in college and through seminary, once a week for about seven years. It didn't matter how many miles I was from home, her love rooted me.[4]"

The people who matter most to us are those who show up in our lives. The people who hurt us the most are those who do not. Those who left us, abandoned us, broke their word, and deserted us - those hurt us more than anyone else. Every person has this innate desire to be "with." We want to be with other people, to know and be known, to live in closeness and community.

This deep need is especially visible in babies. Little ones cry when they wake up and before they go to bed and usually hate being alone. When a parent or family member comes and picks them up, they settle down. We have a strong, innate desire to be with one another.

The children impacted by fatherlessness are accustomed to having authority figures leave – authority figures and dads are a revolving door. Inconsistent, they are here today and gone forever. Not to be trusted.

---

4 Excerpt from: The Heroic Path: In Search of the Masculine Heart, John Sowers, Hachette Books, New York, 2014.

THE MENTORING PROJECT

THOSE WHO MEAN THE MOST TO US ARE THOSE WHO SHOW UP IN OUR LIVES.

@JOHNSOWERS | @TMPROJECT

#MENTOR

But showing up – offering unconditional presence – in the life of a fatherless child creates a new paradigm of hope. It revives and opens space in a child's heart to begin to trust again. When we faithfully show up in the life of another, we say without words, "I am with you."

Showing up echoes the promise of God that says "I am with you."

To me, this is one of the most powerful promises of the Bible – the promise of the presence. Over and over again, God shows his commitment to his people through presence.

- When Joseph was thrown into a well and left for dead, he was sold into slavery, falsely accused of rape, and imprisoned, "the Lord was with Joseph and gave him success in whatever he did." (Genesis 39.23)
- Moses pleaded with God to stay with him and His people, as it appeared Moses might have to go on without His Presence. After Moses pled with God, God promised, "My Presence will go with you and I will give you rest." (Exodus 33.14)
- After Moses passed, his mentee, Joshua, took over the leadership of Israel. Joshua continued Moses' trek towards the promised land. God said to him, "As I was with Moses, so will I be with you. Do not be terrified, do not be discouraged, for the Lord your God will be with you wherever you go." (Joshua 1.5,9)
- King Nebuchadnezzar watched as Shadrach, Meshach and Abednego were thrown into the furnace. The guards were killed by the flames, but another "Man" appeared with the men among the flames. God gave these three men a visible reminder that He was with them, even in the fire. (Daniel 3.22-30)
- When the people of God were captured and exiled by the Babylonians, God kept sending messages and prophecies

> saying He was with them and He had a special plan for them. Jeremiah reminded them, "I am with you and will save you." (Jeremiah 30.11) And God used Isaiah to remind His people, "Fear not for I have redeemed you, I have called you by name, you are mine." (Isaiah 43)

And through the mouth of Isaiah, God delivers the good news that will change history, the music that will never stop, announcing the Coming One who will bring love and peace forever. Isaiah 7.14 says, "Therefore the Lord himself will give you a sign, a virgin will be with child and will give birth to a son, and will call him Immanuel (God with us)."

After his early ministry finished and Christ was crucified, buried and raised, He gave this mandate, "Go and make disciples of all the nations, and surely I am with you always, to the very end of the age." (Matthew 28.19-20)

God's very name captures the importance of presence, Immanuel – "God with us." The heart and intention of God is clear during the miracle of Christmas with the Incarnation of Christ. God has demonstrated a desire for radical with-ness, since the Garden of Eden, when God walked with Adam in the cool of the day. God desires to be close to His people.

What does " God with us" mean for us as mentors?

First, it means that showing up – intentional presence – is rooted in God's promise to us and is the foundation of our mentoring relationship. Our faithful presence echoes God's promise to us, and when we show up for others this way, we echo His promise to them. Showing up is one of the most deeply rooted loving and biblical things we can do for another person. It also reminds us that:

Children care more about our presence than the activities we do with them.

CHILDREN CARE MORE ABOUT OUR PRESENCE THAN THE ACTIVITIES WE DO WITH THEM.

@JOHNSOWERS | @TMPROJECT

#MENTOR

Activities matter, but mentees are far more concerned about being with you than your plans for the afternoon. They want to be with. Some of the best moments happen during the rhythms of everyday life – eating burritos, going to the car wash, talking about school, talking about the highs and lows of the week. Give your mentee time and space to grow. Ask specific questions such as:

1. What was the best thing that happened this week?
2. What was the hardest thing that happened this week?
3. What is your favorite subject? Why?
4. What is your favorite book, movie, song? Why?
5. What would you like to do when you finish school?
6. If you could go anywhere, where would you go? Why?
7. When is your birthday?
8. What kind of man / woman do you want to be? (If silence – start with what they do *not* want to be. Jail. Wasted gifts. Wasted life.)

The best questions cannot be answered with one word. For example, the question "How was school today?" can be answered with one-word responses. "Fine. Good. Okay." On the other hand, a better question is, "What is something you learned for the first time today?"

Generally speaking, boys converse better "side by side" rather than talking "face to face." For example, if a mentor and mentee are shooting free throws, the mentee may be more open to talking than if they were sitting at a coffee shop looking at each other across a table. Girls, on the other hand, may prefer a higher level of eye contact and "face to face" conversing with one another.

Whether you are mentoring a boy or a girl, it is helpful to pursue dialogue with teachers, parents, guardians, grandparents and youth pastors – anyone who can help you "fill in the blanks" of what may be going on in your mentee's life.

Several years ago, my six-year old mentee won a track meet and was awarded a blue ribbon. His mother told me he carried the ribbon in his backpack all week so he could tell me when we hung out on Friday. A few minutes into our time I began to ask him about it. (He didn't volunteer the information.)

> So, your mom told me you ran in a track meet?
> Yes.
> That is great, did you enjoy it?
> Yes.
> Awesome - Did you finish the race?
> Yes.
> That's really great – did you place?
> Yes.
> Did you win?
> Yes.
> Amazing – did you get anything for winning?
> Yes.
> What did you get?
> A ribbon.
> Where is your ribbon?
> My backpack.
> Can I see your ribbon?
> Yes. (reaches into his backpack and pulls it out)
> Great job!!! Well done.

I would have never known about the race or the ribbon or how much he wanted to tell me about it had it not been for his mom telling me. Even when I asked him, he was shy. But he was really proud to show off his ribbon.

Often children don't volunteer information. Even if great or drastic things are happening in their lives, they don't talk about it. By connecting with their parents, keepers, or guardians, we can sometimes find clues about what is happening. Also, they are less likely to communicate struggles. A parent or teacher can tell us if they are struggling with a specific subject in school or being picked on or afraid of something or having another challenge.

Be a student of your mentee's life.

Keep investigating. Stay persistent. What does he care about? What are his dreams? What does he like or dislike? What does he never talk about? What does his relationship with family look like? What does he think about school, or his first job?

A child may or may not be accustomed to speaking with an adult. Build trust slowly over time through shared experiences and meeting once a week or so, for weeks and months and, if possible, years. Don't worry about an initial lack of responsiveness; focus on showing up.

Be physically and emotionally present. Don't look at your smartphone. Don't check your text messages or your email. Be fully there. These first months are building months, and being fully present is the cornerstone of your relationship. Good mentors give full, undistracted attention to their mentee for the duration. Your presence is a gift. Engage in active listening:

- Put away your phone and all distractions.
- Face your mentee.
- Be open. Be sensitive and aware.
- Don't cross your arms. Don't lean away or to the side.
- Notice their body language.
- Reflect what your mentee is feeling – reflect it in your eyes.
- Repeat what your mentee said and ask clarifying questions.

One of my mentors, Bill, listened to me talk for hours. We would drive together to hunt or fish or work on his cabin and Bill would ask direct questions and listen with endless patience, as I thought and processed ideas out loud. His focused attention said to me, without words, "You are important. What you are saying is important. I value you."

Bill created opportunities – he created space – so he could listen to me. He took me along for errands and scheduled low-key activities, activities that would allow us to process and talk. Most of what I was looking for was affirmation, not answers. Bill did that so well. He sprinkled in short, encouraging remarks like "Well, that sounds good – great job!"

Mentees are not usually looking for advice, but affirmation.

They want someone to listen to them, value them, care for them and be proud of them. They sometimes want guidance and advice, but almost every time they are actually looking for affirmation. And listening allows you to show up for your mentee in this way. Ask yourself the following questions

During our social exchanges, do I talk or listen more?
Am I really listening or am I more focused on what I am going to say next?
Am I making meaningful eye contact or am I distracted?
Am I listening for understanding for more information, or am I listening to "offer advice" or correct or judge?
Am I a safe person for my mentee to speak with?

A seasoned mentor allows the mentee to "have the ball" in conversations by thinking of his / her needs first. The gift of presence requires us to be other-aware.

The wise mentor follows Romans 12:15: he "rejoices with those who rejoice, he mourns with those who mourn." A mentor who is fully present reflects emotions and experiences of her mentee. Not only does listening

MENTEES ARE NOT USUALLY LOOKING FOR ADVICE, BUT FOR AFFIRMATION.

@JOHNSOWERS | @TMPROJECT

#MENTOR

communicate that a mentee is important – but it gives the mentor a chance to get to know the mentee, to affirm and encourage him / her in ways that are meaningful to the mentee.

Food for Thought:

Who showed up faithfully for you?
Who listened to you – gave you time and attention? How did that change you?
How did it shape you into who you are today?
How can you take that into your mentoring relationship?

Your mentoring relationship (like all relationships) grows in stages. You build trust and develop communication. Slowly it evolves into a two way relationship. Many high-risk youth have a hard time with trusting, and it takes time to develop. They experience inconsistency and broken promises. This is especially true when youth are from fatherless or unstable backgrounds where adults have disappointed them. Mentors can expect:

- Missed appointments
- A lack of responsiveness
- Unreasonable requests
- Possible outlandish "testing" behavior
- A lack of positive feedback from the mentee

High-risk youth have layers of defensiveness and protection. You may not feel (or hear) any positive feedback. The child may simply not know how to express gratitude, or may not be able to say he / she enjoys your friendship. Many children raised in a home while mom works three jobs are not equipped to share and appreciate. You may feel grossly unappreciated, while the opposite is true.

Another young man I mentored was quiet – barely talkative for the first six months. I had no idea if he enjoyed having a mentor or not. He seemed indifferent, even when I celebrated his birthday, brought lunch to school and worked hard to help him feel accepted. It wasn't until months later, when I met his birth-mom, who was so excited to meet me, that it became clear that he appreciated our time together. She had been hearing about me all along and was grateful for me, even though her son had never once said thanks. It was a strange dynamic, but then I realized many of these children do not know how to express themselves.

Remember that many children do not trust authority – or any adults - since they have been betrayed and left. They live in unpredictable and sometimes unstable and hostile environments. Some of them even experience trauma, gang violence, threats and bullying. Adults in their household may come and go, and many of these children are just waiting for you to do the same thing.

This is why we emphasize again and again: mentors win by showing up.

8

CHILDREN ASPIRE TO BE WHAT THEY SEE.

@JOHNSOWERS | @TMPROJECT

#MENTOR

Tool Two: Live Out
Chapter Eight

In two of our The Mentoring Project Partner Sites, we recruit and train mentors to serve alongside the Police Department working with high-risk youth. It is a great partnership because the Police work with the interventions and youth struggling with truancy. They do the intervention and invite the youth into the opportunity, and then we recruit and train and match the mentors.

When we first started working with the youth once a week, we asked them the infamous question, "What do you want to be when you grow up?"

Every child answered, "A basketball player, singer, rapper, athlete, famous."

We showed up for them for several months. We spent time with them, got to know them, mentored them and did life together. After that, we asked them the same question again, "What do you want to be when you grow up?" This time their answer was very different. They said, "Police Officers and Mentors."

Children aspire to be what they see.

But if no one lays out a vision for their future, the only future they can dream or imagine is the future they see right in front of them. Every person dreams of a hopeful future, a life of significance, of meaning, of relationships with people we love and who love us in return. If children do not see this at home, they look to outside influences to fill this dream void.

And what are they seeing? Musicians on the radio or internet. Athletes on television. Friends on social media. Social media and television have become the moral construct for this generation. Social media and television have great potential for good. But they were never intended to raise fatherless or orphan children.

This is why modeling – setting a good visual example – is so critical.

People retain nearly twice as much of what they see versus what they hear. This is especially true of children. The child you mentor will watch you closely. Listen to what you say. Watch your actions, attitudes and responses. Sometimes you will be aware of it, but most of the times you will not. The first way to build trust is to show up faithfully – and deeper trust is built when you are a trustworthy model.

Children watch us closely and then absorb what they see like a sponge. The values we live. The beliefs we hold. The convictions we show. You can learn a great deal about a person by listening to their conversations, watching their actions, seeing how they react to life and respond to adversity.

Mentoring is a neutral term.

We can mentor people towards evil or towards good. A gang leader can be a very effective mentor. Granted, he is mentoring young children towards destruction and violence and drugs and death. But many gang leaders are effective mentors. We can mentor someone to be a mechanic or to be good at spelling or to build bikes. Mentoring is neutral, and this begins the question:

What are we mentoring people to become?

In I Corinthians 11.1, Paul writes, "Imitate me as I imitate Christ."

Christ is our example. He is our goal. All of us become like whoever or whatever we follow. We become like whatever we set our hearts and affections on. This is why Scripture constantly calls us to "set our hearts on

THE MENTORING PROJECT

MENTORING IS A NEUTRAL TERM.

@JOHNSOWERS | @TMPROJECT

#MENTOR

things above" and "fix our eyes on Christ." As we follow Him and focus on Him, we become more and more like Him. This is why our active, living relationship with Christ is so vital. Remember, who you are is who they become.

For the purpose of relational mentoring, we emphasize these three core values:

Humility. Integrity. Sincerity.

HUMILITY

Philippians 2:3 says, "In humility, consider others better than yourself." Humility is the idea of thinking of another person first. In the words of CS Lewis, "Humility is not thinking less of yourself, it is thinking of yourself less."

Humility – being other centered – is the best way to express value to another person. Humility says: "Who you are is important and what you say is important, so I will consider you first, I listen to you first, I will put your needs first. You matter."

A recent *USA Today*[5] study identifies "Fame and Wealth" as the top goals for Generation Y. Whereas children of previous generations wanted to grow up and be doctors, lawyers, nurses, firemen, professors, children of this generation want to be noticed and exalted above their peers.

For the selfie-generation, online posturing, appearance and image trump character, substance and honor. Children are racing to social media to do outrageous things, no matter how scandalous or shameful, for "fifteen minutes of fame." As you model humility, you are a genuine contrast to almost everything else a child is seeing.

When you model humility, you fly in the face of a generation who wants to grow up to become famous. You are a stark contrast to all of the social

5 "Generation Y's Goal? Wealth and Fame," USA Today, by Sharon Jayson, January 10, 2007.

media posturing, the stratification between who is cool and what is not. Instead of shouting, you are quiet and instead of caring about the pecking order, you defer. Proverbs wisely says, “Humility comes before honor.” (Proverbs 18.12)

Humility is such a precious commodity that anyone who has it stands out in the crowd. It is a bold contrast to the online bragging and photo ops. For so many, social media has become the place of stratification, of standing on the shoulders of another to be different, to be above, to be better. Proverbs 27.2 says, “Let another praise you and not your own lips.”

One man who models humility is NFL Hall of Fame Coach Tony Dungy. Tony spoke at one of our mentor recruiting events, and he showed up early, with his children. Instead of retreating to the green room or asking for anything, he asked us, “How can I serve you?”

Then Coach Dungy spent an hour talking to mentors and children and supporters. After that he spoke to a large audience for 50 minutes and then made his way to the book table outside. Once there, he spoke to everyone who waited in line to talk with him. He met and talked to people for over two hours. By then, it was late in the day and he was tired. However, he looked at us and said, “What’s next?”

Coach Dungy relentlessly served us and mentors and children for hours. Even when we were done, he was not. He kept looking for an opportunity to serve.

Food for Thought:

Who modeled humility for you? How did that impact you?

How did Christ model humility for us? (See Philippians 2:3-11)

In what ways can you model humility as a mentor?

INTEGRITY

Integrity is being the same, inside and out. It is having a sense of wholeness and completeness and being incorruptible. Christ, our perfect model of integrity, always did exactly what He said He would do, no matter how hard or painful. He was perfectly trustworthy and dependable. He never promised anything that didn't happen. He made good on everything He said He would do.

Mentors must also model integrity.

Integrity is tantamount to building trust. Integrity is a building term which means having sound and unimpaired condition. Integrity is the foundation of our relationships. If a building does not have a good foundation or loses integrity, it crumbles. It may look good on the outside, but if the walls are deplaning or the foundation is cracking, the entire building will come down.

We must align our words and deeds. We must make sure we are exactly who we say we are and do the right thing, even when no one is looking. Proverbs 13.6 adds, "Righteousness guards the man of integrity."

Integrity is alignment of word and deed, flesh and marrow, heart and action, intention and completion, audience and solitude.

We must have integrity with our words; our "yes" must be "yes" and our "no" must be "no." The children we mentor will hang on our words and promises, and we need to be careful not to ever make promises we cannot keep. We must also have integrity with our actions and reactions. We must watch the way we drive our car and react to other drivers, the way we treat and relate to others. Those around us tend to learn more from what is caught than what is taught. They are watching and learning.

THE MENTORING PROJECT

INTEGRITY IS ALIGNMENT OF WORD AND DEED, FLESH AND MARROW, HEART AND ACTION, INTENTION AND COMPLETION, AUDIENCE AND SOLITUDE.

@JOHNSOWERS | @TMPROJECT

#MENTOR

If we do not keep our word, we will become another undependable authority figure in the revolving door of authority figures. This is perhaps the worst thing we can do. In the end, this person does more harm than good and builds yet another call us on a hopeful young heart.

A few years ago, my mentee asked if we could go to Chuck E. Cheese's and play Skee Ball. I told him we might be able to go the next week if he did well in school and his mom said it was okay. The next week rolled around, and I picked him up but had forgotten my promise. Then his mom reminded me, "He has been waiting all week for Chuck E. Cheese's and did well in school this week. He is looking forward to it!" So after a quick trip to the bank, we went to Chuck E.Cheese's. I'm grateful for his mom in that situation and how involved she was in the process.

Food for Thought:

Who in your life modeled integrity?
Did it make you feel they were trustworthy and dependable?
Did others over-promise and under-deliver? How did those people make you feel?
How can you live with integrity in a way that builds trust?

SINCERITY

Along with humility and integrity, **a mentor must model sincerity.**

The word "sincerity" comes from a Latin word meaning "without wax," and it was a pottery term. Pottery would often crack when fired in the oven, and most cracked pottery was thrown away, but some dishonest dealers would fill the cracks with colored wax and pretend that the pieces were whole. Sincere pots had no wax, and any cracks showed.

Living with sincerity means living honestly.

This is a perfect balance to integrity because it allows for grace. If we only talk about integrity, we could be tempted to cover up our mistakes. But if we live honestly, we are not afraid to appropriately show our cracks. This vulnerability can be very encouraging to others, as it says, "I am like you."

All relationships are formed around two people living honestly.

If one or both parties is somehow ashamed or afraid to share, this lack of honesty will create an artificial environment, and the conversations and relationship will stay at the surface level. Deep trust will never be formed, and transformation will not occur. As mentors, we lead the depth of the conversation and the ensuing relationship. Of course this takes time, but as we open ourselves to another person, we lead and create a safe environment. The other person subconsciously believes, "If this person is willing to share with me, they trust me, and maybe I can trust them, too."

So many people are afraid to live honestly because they might be rejected, they might lose a relationship, a parent, friends, or their reputation, or they might be confused as being weak. This is why mentors must lead the way in living honestly and *extending grace* to others whenever they live honestly around us. Once we create a safe place, we may be shocked what a mentee decides to share with us.

We create a grace-environment and show others humility when we apologize, admit our wrongdoing and resolve to do better next time. We are called to live without wax, but not without cracks. Cracks are evidence of grace in our lives. Once a trusting relationship is built, mentors can share (appropriate) levels of their own struggles or issues. Mentors can lead with vulnerability, opening up about a work challenge or a previous school or college challenge.

Also, we don't have to share only our struggles. A mentor can let a mentee "in" on a decision-making process, walking through the pros and cons and the long-term ramifications and options. Decision-making is a valuable skill. If a mentor is open and lives honestly, a mentee can learn by living honestly with a mentor. With good questions, patience and exploration, a mentor can help a mentee walk through decision-making processes with school, relationships with the opposite sex, first jobs or college.

One of the best ways we teach others is by allowing them to see us working through issues. This is a far different posture than preaching or lecturing or sermonizing at someone. It is tempting to give someone a lecture about an issue. It is quite another thing to open up about how this decision affected you personally.

- Example of lecturing: “You really should try harder at math. If you fail math, you won’t pass 8th grade.”
- Example of personal sharing: “Math was hard for me too. Especially algebra. I had to stay after school and work with the math teacher to get a C grade. I worked for hours. It wasn’t my best subject but I got the grade and passed. ”

Which of those two examples is more powerful and effective? When you have the courage to be honest and share your personal struggles, it is a powerful teacher.

A mentee needs a stable, trusting and safe environment to thrive. The mentee is unsure what and how to share. Even more importantly, he doesn’t know how well he will be received. Some youth are open, others are more guarded, and some are completely closed off.

Food For Thought:

Who modeled sincerity for you? Who lived honestly?
Did that encourage you? How did it make you respond?
What did their honesty do for your relationship?
Who showed you grace when you struggled?
How did that grace transform you?

A MENTOR MUST MODEL SINCERITY. LIVING WITH SINCERITY MEANS LIVING HONESTLY.

@JOHNSOWERS | @TMPROJECT

#MENTOR

9

TRANSFORMATION RIDES IN THE BACKSEAT OF RELATIONSHIP

@JOHNSOWERS | @TMPROJECT

#MENTOR

Tool Three: Speak In Chapter Nine

Speaking into another person's life – coaching – comes after trust is established.

This opportunity usually comes after trust has been established over time. If we show up unconditionally and faithfully, live out with humility, integrity and sincerity, we may earn the right to be heard. We believe these relational building blocks are the best way to transform and influence another. Over time, we are given the sacred trust to speak into another person's life.

Transformation rides in the backseat of relationship.

This "speaking in" comes in the other person's timeframe. He has to open the door. Sometimes this opens quickly, but other times it may take years. When we are allowed to finally walk into these places, we have been given sacred and vulnerable access and must "tread lightly there."

When Christ came in the flesh, John said he was "full of grace and truth." John 1.14. We must embody both of these things. If we are imbalanced, too heavy on one and not the other, we miss it. We all know examples of both. The football coach that is 100% truth, yelling at his players. Or the person who never creates any "friction" because he /she is too scared to say anything with edges.

We must speak in with grace and truth.

Many children who have been burned by authority figures may be surprisingly fragile, closed off, overly emotional or especially defensive. They may shut themselves off to any and all instruction. This is why we must speak with an abundance of grace, because any correction may actually feel like rejection.

It was this way for me. Whenever a principal or sports coach corrected me, it felt like a personal rejection. It was not in my understanding to hear someone say something to me that was disapproving but still loving. I couldn't understand that. Disapproval was very personal and in my mind it was always attached to rejection. I couldn't understand that a coach or teacher could correct me while still approving of me as a person.

Because of this, it was hard to relate to authority figures. I lived in fear around them. I was a "show pony" and worked hard for their approval. I lived this way well into my twenties. Do you approve of me? Do you think well of me? Did you see what I just did; am I lovable now?

Many fatherless youth see the world this same way. Because of this rejection, we need to be extra affirming and lavish in our encouragement. And even when we do offer correction, it needs to be gentle and wrapped with encouragement.

At the same time, we must resist the temptation to avoid the truth. It will be easier to "let things slide" and ignore the things we must speak about. Our role as mentors is not to be a counselor or therapist or someone who must fix our mentee. But we must speak with grace and truth, and we must not shrink back from telling the whole truth. We must be sensitive while not holding back.

In the course of your mentoring relationship, there will be small windows of opportunities – rare moments – afforded you to speak into the life of your mentee. These are almost always totally unexpected. You will be hanging out at school, or on the way to the ballgame or on the phone, and something will come up. Good coaches are always looking and listening for the teachable moments. In a one-to-one relationship, we can apply specific truth to someone's specific context.

This is the difference between the fun uncle and the truthful coach. The fun uncle just hangs out, plays games, laughs, tells jokes, entertains. Many mentors just see themselves as the fun uncle, and never speak truth into the life of their mentee. The truthful coach also does all of those fun things but also speaks up when the opportunity is at hand.

Don't shy away from these moments. Your short, well-timed words can make a lasting impact. It is in these moments that we have a rare chance to say something loving and encouraging that may change the course of our mentee's life. **Speaking into a child's life changes the trajectory of who he becomes.**

Jesus is our example. He was the balance of saying the hard things while still being perfectly tender and infinitely graceful. He never shrank from the truth – but He never wielded it carelessly. He said and did radical things, but in His heart, He loved people. He didn't chide them but came alongside them tenderly as a friend. And Jesus reminded us that sometimes the most loving thing we can do is say hard things.

One of the ways we can speak in is to *identify gifts and talents.*

Simply identifying and naming someone's gifts and talents can be life-changing. Many children don't know what they are good at, and they are still learning what gives them joy and how they were created. The verse "Train a child the way he should go" (Proverbs 22.6) has the sense that we are to train up a child in their "created bent." Each child has unique gifts and skills, and a mentor helps call those out and shape them.

In the Old Testament, this was called "the Blessing," as part of the adult initiation rites. A father would bless his son by calling out his gifts and talents. This "calling out" was a key component of the blessing. The father would not project his dreams onto his son but would draw out his created gifts and purposes.

Millions of children never hear the words, “I believe in you and I’m proud of you.” They remain stuck with insecurity, unable to assert themselves with confidence at school or home, or later in work and marriage. Their role models are in media, on television and the radio. Famous athletes, singers, actors. Many of these children don’t know where they will be tomorrow, let alone next year.

Our words have power of life and death (Proverbs 18.21). Our words of blessing can override words of cursing, of disappointment and discouragement, and can fill the voids left by neglect, absence, shame or rejection. In these critical moments of blessing, a child hears,

“I believe in you. I’m proud of you.”

When a child hears these words, he gains courage and confidence. He begins to believe – maybe for the first time in his life – that he is good at something. He begins to gain vision for his life. A blueprint. He begins to see something else for his future, in his mind and his imagination, perhaps for the first time – who he is called to be and who he can become.

The Mentoring Project Founder, Donald Miller, shares about his own mentor, David Gentiles. Don grew up fatherless, and while his mom was very supportive and did her best, Don was headed down the wrong paths. By junior high, Don was breaking into houses and stealing things. One day, a man named David Gentiles invited him to a literary group. Don didn’t care about going but he wanted to impress David.

Later, David identified Don as a good writer and gave him a spot to write in the weekly youth bulletin. David “spoke in” and named Don as a writer – and writing is still a big part of Don’s identity today. Since then, Don has written several books, including three New York Times bestsellers, and has dramatically changed the voice and scope of faith-based books.

SPEAKING INTO A CHILD'S LIFE CHANGES THE TRAJECTORY OF WHO HE BECOMES.

@JOHNSOWERS | @TMPROJECT

#MENTOR

David died several years ago and Don did the Eulogy at his funeral. Hundreds of people showed up. That night after the funeral, Don wrote a blog called "The Best Sermon I've Ever Heard." He wrote:

> *Blue Like Jazz* was dedicated to David Gentiles, because David is the reason I am a writer. He was a remarkable human being. I heard somebody say every life is a sermon, that every new day we preach a point.
>
> If this is true, David Gentiles preached the best sermon I've ever heard. I'll never forget him, or what he did with his life. David was a rock of a man and his sermon was love. His life and what it pointed toward will remain with me, and no doubt with many of you, as a foundation on which you will build your families, your friendships and your faith. It's hard to imagine a sermon on love has ever been said better. I learned more about Jesus from David than any other person I know.
>
> In a culture where professional ministers are tempted to use people to build churches, David Gentiles used the church to get to people. Sunday morning was a trick that got us in the room so we could share our lives. He didn't care about buildings or salaries or status, he cared about us. That's why hundreds of us have come today to fill this stadium, to say goodbye to a very simple man who never wrote a book or recorded an album, who never put his name on a marquee over a church, or sold his sermons on the internet. We are here because we have been loved personally by David Gentiles. For some of us, at some point in our lives, he may have been the only one.
>
> David asked me to write a guest column for the youth-group newsletter, a publication that went out to about fifty people, printed on the Xerox machine behind the church secretary's desk. But it didn't matter to me. I was published. David couldn't have been more proud of me. When people ask today why I am a writer, I

tell them about David Gentiles, about how if it weren't for David, I doubt I would have ever been introduced to books, or started writing in the first place. I write today because when I was a kid it made David Gentiles proud.

When I found out David had passed, I grieved the fact I wouldn't have him to turn to whenever I do something good. He's the first person I want to tell, because he never reprimanded you for bragging, he only laughed and squinted his eyes and told you that you did good. I never knew how much that meant to me until it was taken away. I often wondered why David never wrote a book of his own. He had enormous talent and a heart that networked effortlessly amongst the marginalized and the powerful alike. He could have sold a million books, but he was too busy showing up for others.

His sermon, then, was Christ.

It's clear now. Like Christ, he created the church to get to people. He never wrote a book. He leaves behind no home, and few possessions. His passing was untimely and seemingly unjust. He spent his life ushering people home, standing in as a father, a shepherd, a brother and a friend. It's our only comfort, then, that David and Christ are together now. They have everything in common.[6]

Food For Thought:

Who "saw you" and called you into a special future?
Who blessed you and spoke into your life with grace and truth?
Have you had the opportunity to "speak into" the lives of others?

6 Donald Miller, "The Best Sermon I Ever Heard, Remembering David Gentiles," storylineblog.com, 12.30.2009.

10

Tools: Nuts and Bolts Chapter Ten

This chapter covers some practical ideas you can take into a mentoring relationship, as well as conversation topics, questions and other helpful "on-ramps" for building your relationship. These "nuts and bolts" are practical tips to help you hold your relationship together.

Remember that the safety of a child is always first. Make sure you are extra cautious in every activity, wearing seatbelts and necessary protective gear. All mentors must go through background checks and be in contact with the respective program coordinators.

The best sustainable mentoring relationships are proximity-sensitive. It is unrealistic to think you will drive an hour each way to see your mentee every week. Ideally, a mentee can live 15 minutes or less from you, or the school or church or site where you mentor is less than a 15 minute drive.

In your relationship, remember:

- Be flexible, persistent and patient.
- Set expectations and hold boundaries.
- Mentoring often works best when mentor and mentee have an agreed time and day of the week. Mentoring becomes a rhythm.
- Appreciate your differences. Don't be intimidated or worry about the differences, such as being up on the latest music or vocabulary or style. Just show up faithfully.

- Have the courage to take advantage of "teachable moments."
- Allow mentees in on your decision-making processes, and let them learn the skill.

It is not appropriate to:

- Take or talk about drugs or alcohol before or during your time with your mentee.
- Take sides in a family dispute.
- Physically discipline your mentee in any way, or use guilt or shame or the "silent treatment."
- Make inappropriate jokes, or hurtful or embarrassing or derogatory comments with your mentee.
- Touch your mentee in any way other than a high-five, fist bump, or give your mentee a quick "side-hug" if he or she initiates.

As in any new relationship, there may be questions, doubts, or insecurities as you begin to get to know each other. Here are some thoughts to guide you through a few common obstacles you may encounter while developing a mentoring relationship. You don't have to be stylish and cool and superhuman to make a difference. Just show up. Be available and present.

Children are more concerned about your presence than your abilities.

Don't lose interest if you don't see immediate or early "returns." Many mentors lose interest if the relationship is not rewarding and withdraw, spending less time with their mentee. It is important to remember that your greatest blessing may come in the time you give and the life you model. Give unconditionally, without seeking anything in return. Be patient and remember that mentoring is slow. Mentoring takes time.

You may feel pressure about a mentee's expectations and wonder if you are measuring up. Don't feel insecure; just go back over the tools and

THE MENTORING PROJECT

CHILDREN ARE MORE CONCERNED ABOUT YOUR PRESENCE THAN YOUR ABILITIES.

@JOHNSOWERS | @TMPROJECT

#MENTOR

ask yourself: Am I showing up faithfully? Am I modeling Christ? Am I speaking in during the teachable moments? Feel free to communicate with your mentees and ask them about expectations. You will likely find that your expectations are much higher and more specific than theirs.

Look for common interests.

This is a conversation that needs to happen during the matching process. What does your mentee like? Soccer? Art? Guitar? These common interests are connecting points, and they give you something to talk about and participate in together. Again, many children – especially boys – learn best "side by side." They will talk more when they are playing catch than when they are sitting across the table looking at you.

FAQ:

My mentee does not like to talk. How do I get him / her to talk and open up?

First of all, this is normal. Do not be discouraged. Ask specific questions. Ask about things you know they are interested in. Then ask some other questions: "What was the best thing that happened to you this week? What was the worst thing? What is one thing you would change about yourself? What are your biggest strengths? If someone gave you a million dollars, how would you spend it?"

After these initial questions ask follow up questions that repeat what mentees said. "So you are saying you would buy a house for your mom? Awesome. What would the house be like? Where would it be located? Why would you buy her a house?" Remember the answers.

We've been hanging out a few months, and it barely seems like we have made progress. What do I do?

At The Mentoring Project, we talk about the six-month hill. Any relationship, and especially one with an at-risk or high-risk child, may take several monthsto build. Keep showing up, modeling Christ and speaking encouragement. The first six months are building months, and they are formative for the long-term relationship.

<u>My mentee sometimes skips out and stands me up. What do I do?</u>

This sometimes happens. Don't get discouraged. Most of the time, a mentee is either testing you or simply lacks the social or organizational skills to plan and remember. This is why he needs a mentor! In rare cases, a mentee is simply not committed to the mentoring relationship. Your program coordinator will help you in this situation, talking with the child and the parents and, in extremely rare cases, may need to help you find another child to mentor.

<u>My mentee and I don't click. What do I do?</u>

There will be times when you feel you are not connecting. This is normal as well. Remember, there is a great chance that you may be from completely different backgrounds and cultures. His childhood as an eighth grader barely resembles anything you knew in junior high. Also, be sure not to expect much back in return. Keep the mindset of a servant – give, give, give. Over time the fruit of your labor may be rewarded.

Also, it is our experience that some mentees push you to see if you will stay around. Understand that children who have been hurt or rejected or have been through some type of trauma construct heavy defense mechanisms for survival. As you show up faithfully, over time, the child should begin to lower his/her defenses. If your uneasiness persists, we encourage you to speak with your program coordinator to find a working solution. Whatever you decide, please approach this situation with great care, as the child may have already been through a great deal of rejection.

<u>How do I deal with my mentee making poor choices?</u>

You will never agree with all of the choices he makes. And if you shame him or heap guilt on him because of these choices, you may do damage. You will create a false construct and make the child far less likely to ever open up again. He will see you as someone he must "perform" for and will decide to be an actor around you.

It is important that children understand that all choices have ramifications – some are good and some are not. Galatians 6:6-9 says, "A man reaps what he sows." Choices involving disrespect of authority, lying, cheating, stealing and mistreatment of others are building a foundation of character. He is becoming those choices.

On the other hand, make sure to praise and encourage good choices, such as studying for a test, responding in a situation with honor, walking away from a fight, not cheating, going to school. Whatever choices a child is making, he is becoming his choices. Sometimes all it takes is to ask questions, "How did that choice work out?" "Would you have chosen differently if you could do it again?" "If you keep making that choice for the next ten years, where will it lead you?"

One of your most important jobs is to create a safe place for your mentee to be honest, with good and bad choices. Poor choices are a great place – if trust is in place – for you to speak into his life. They are also good opportunities for teachable moments (without heavy lecturing) for you to share how you handled different choices in your life and how you overcame poor choices.

Physical Touch and Safety Boundaries

Respecting physical boundaries shows a mentee and their parents that you are safe and trustworthy. You must respect their personal space and privacy. Examples of appropriate touch are brief and infrequent physical contact initiated by mentee, such as: side hugs, high fives, pats on the shoulder or hand, fist bumps.

Examples of inappropriate touch are physical contact initiated by the mentor, full frontal hugs or other types of touch not listed above under "appropriate touch," and any violation of laws against sexual contact between adults and children.

On rare occasion, your mentee may initiate inappropriate physical contact with you. When this occurs, we expect that you will make every effort to redirect that contact in a way that is consistent with The Mentoring Project and Partner Organization policies. For example, if your mentee greets you with a full frontal hug at the beginning of your session, you can move this contact into a side hug or keep the contact as brief as possible. It is a good idea to talk with your mentee about the exchange in order to avoid hurt feelings and to remind them about The Mentoring Project policy on safe touch.

Boundary Setting

When entering your mentoring relationship, be aware of your personal boundaries (i.e., things you're comfortable talking about and sharing with your mentee). This will be especially important in the area of discipline as what you do and do not tolerate. It is very likely that the mentee will push your boundaries with their actions and words. Like most youth, a mentee will test you. Stay calm. Be patient. Explain, with ample grace, why this behavior is or is not appropriate. Mentoring is not a "quick fix," but a long walk.

Self-Disclosure

As the mentoring relationship progresses, you may choose to disclose information about yourself on sensitive issues. If you choose to disclose something, remember to keep your response general and brief. Do not dwell on dark pasts or be too specific in the details. Be careful not to glorify your struggles. Then make sure you have a conversation about what you've disclosed and what your mentee has learned.

MENTORING IN SPECIFIC CONTEXTS

PART THREE

11

Mentoring Within Specific Communities: Overview Chapter Eleven

One of the goals of The Mentoring Project is to help networks create *"sustainable mentoring communities."*

We believe that mentoring is best done in community. Your church liaisons and your pastor will help encourage this community and keep it thriving.

Mentors have a better chance of winning when they mentor together.

Mentors who have a community are able to help one another and support one another. A mentoring community based in an established community also provides some stability for the children being mentored. If a mentor moves away or has to stop mentoring for any reason, an established community usually has a pool of potential mentors to draw from so that a child is not left without a mentor. Church communities promote mentor sustainability and commitment, which ultimately leads to better relationships.

Mentoring in a group community setting also takes pressure off the mentors.

They no longer have to plan every detail of the meeting. Sometimes they can just show up and participate in the group activity. Churches are natural conduits for these types of mentoring communities to grow and develop. Often, a church or faith community already offers planned events on a weekly or monthly basis. Sometimes they may already have an after-school program. These existing programs serve as doorway opportunities for a mentor to spend time with his mentee.

We have seen dozens of small groups of 8-10 people mentor together. Mentoring becomes a common connecting point, as these mentors often gather together and spend time in prayer and fellowship, sharing their experiences with one another. This is the best case scenario, when a group of men form a "band of brothers" and become a "sustainable mentoring community." This section is devoted to the idea of mentoring in community as well as mentoring in specific contexts, such as foster care, literacy programs, and the urban core.

12

Mentoring within Foster Care Chapter Twelve

There are roughly 400,000 children in foster care in the US at any given time. They have been removed from their families not through any fault of their own but because those who should have cared for them did not or could not.

Jedd Medefind
President, Christian Alliance for Orphans (CAFO)

Mentoring a child in foster care is often a transformative and stabilizing experience for the mentee. A child in foster care may change home addresses, parents, siblings, schools, churches and routines at a dizzying speed. A committed mentor can be their rock – the one who remains constant in a sea of chaos. In the tempest that is foster care, a mentor is a strong anchor.

Imagine the confusion of having a case-worker – an unknown stranger – arrive at your home or school and take you away from your mom or dad… immediately. Now imagine being separated from your siblings, as well as your parents and grandparents. These children enter foster "care" alone and defensive, afraid and confused. Sadly, this transition is usually not a one-time experience.

If a foster care family is not a "fit," children may be pushed from one home to another. Sometimes children are returned to their parents and later removed again. Home placements may change up to ten times (or many more) before a child ages out of the system. Teenagers who never find a permanent home are thrust into adulthood alone.

Think of the family network that supported you through childhood, the teen years and into adulthood. What if you never had a constant character who shared your memories? Who could you trust when relationships failed again and again? Who could you open up to? Who did you admire? Who would you be vulnerable with if you believed you were unlovable?

A committed mentor can be a beacon for a child in foster care – the one constant who shows up week after week to affirm and encourage. A mentor is a positive and dependable adult role model who is rarely "taken away" from a mentee at a moment's notice. The mentor's presence communicates to the mentee that he or she is in fact lovable. Feeling wanted when you are shuffled from house to house or told you are a burden is a breath of fresh air for mentees.

Mentoring a child in foster care requires an "advanced" commitment from the mentor. As compared to a traditional community-based mentoring experience, mentoring a young person in foster care often has more complicating factors: the matching process typically takes much longer, there are more adults who have input regarding the child's care and commitments, the young person may be moved to another home or school without notice to the child or anyone else. A committed mentor for a foster care participant is one who commits not only to show up week after week, but also to do the leg work to "find" the mentee when there is a guardian or housing change. A faithful mentor will be the plumb line that anchors a childhood or the whirl of the teenage years.

Children in foster care may have experienced more pain and disappointment than other children their age. They often build a "tough" exterior that presents as extreme apathy or hardened nonchalance. The mentor of a young person in foster care must truly be "others focused" because the mentee's appreciation for the mentor may not be displayed outwardly for a very long time.

Starting a Mentoring Initiative Alongside Foster Care

When starting a new mentoring initiative for children in foster care, it is crucial to conduct extensive preparation before recruiting mentors. We recommend piloting one to five mentors for one year before attempting a larger recruitment effort. Foster care protocols differ not only from city to city, but even from agency to agency within the same zip code.

Consequently, it is impossible for The Mentoring Project to present a cookie-cutter plan that will work in each foster care environment. What we can offer are helpful guidelines gleaned from our more than five years of mentoring experience. Using our guidelines will help you save time so that you start and climb in a positive direction.

First and most important, the leadership of a new mentoring initiative must get to know and earn the trust of the case workers who will be facilitating the foster care side of the mentor/mentee match. Presenting a new mentoring initiative, while likely a huge positive for the children, will increase the workload demands placed on caseworkers. Start by serving. How can you put together a community to support the caseworkers or agency so that there is room in their day or week to add this new task?

Our favorite example of serving the local foster care caseworkers and agencies is The Forgotten Initiative. You can gain great understanding from The Forgotten Initiative on how to serve a local foster care agency at www.theforgotteninitiative.org.

One way The Forgotten Initiative serves local agencies is by doing mini-makeovers of agency visitation rooms. These visitation rooms are the places children must wait, often alone, while a case worker makes frantic phone calls to find a temporary home for the child. These rooms become a temporary "bedroom" if a home is not found before bedtime. Due to budget restraints, these rooms often may feel more like a holding cell than a welcome respite. The Forgotten Initiative connects the church to the agency to make the visitation rooms a soft landing, a place where children can feel both safe and relaxed.

How can you earn the trust of your local foster care agency? Your mentoring initiative will have a much broader scope if you can offer heightened community care for foster children *and their case workers.*

Once you have earned the trust of your local foster care agency, you need to work with an office decision maker to guide you through the process of becoming an approved source of mentors. You will need to provide detailed information on your mentor interview process, background check and follow up protocols, and accountability for mentee safety.

After you have earned the privilege of being an approved mentor referral partner, you are ready to recruit and train mentors. Gather your interested mentors to attend a mentor training based on The Mentoring Project's Mentor Field Guide and small group training videos. When potential mentors fully understand the relational principles of show up, live out and speak in, they are ready to proceed to mentor interviews, applications and your vetting process. Upon clearing a thorough vetting process, mentors are ready to engage with the secondary vetting process overseen by the foster care agency.

A prepared leader will fully understand the foster care agency's vetting process and have all paperwork ready for a potential mentor to fill out before contacting the foster care agency. It is helpful to work with your local foster care agency to develop a target timeline for completing paperwork, background checks, interview or any other steps in the matching process as required by the foster care agency. Make sure your mentors understand and accept this timeline before moving forward in the process. We suggest an advocate who stays in touch with the case workers to gently remind them of the pending mentor match, offering help and encouragement.

This advocate should be Cced on any e-mail communications between a potential mentor and the foster care agency. Then if any forms are lost or misplaced within "the system," the mentor advocate will have a back up copy.

To avoid mentor disillusionment, take care to build a sustainable mentor community that offers monthly care for your mentors as well. The Mentoring Project provides blueprints and consulting for mentor care to organizations who are members of its National Mentor Alliance (e-mail advocate@thementoringproject.org to learn more). Additionally, individual mentors can join The Mentoring Project's Mentor Collective to receive monthly opt-in resources to continually equip mentors for their mentor journey (join via tmp.webconnex.com/mentorcollective).

Mentoring within Foster Care

Before starting a mentoring relationship with a child or teenager connected to the foster care system, the mentor is committed to an extended vetting process. This extended process is beneficial but tedious. Please remember that these children have already been neglected or violated by an adult. The process should be very thorough in finding safe and reliable mentors. Each agency process is different, but a general rule of thumb is to be prepared to stay fast through a six to nine-month process. Most of the time this vetting process will not be a smooth train ride. It will be more like a bumpy pony-express with starts and stops, redirects and do-overs. Remember that the case worker facilitating your match is likely overwhelmed and understaffed. Ideally, you will have an advocate nudging the match process along.

While the foster care agency may be slow to move to the next step in the vetting and matching process, the ideal mentor within foster care will tenaciously meet deadlines and fully complete all requested forms. Again, each time you send an e-mail communication to the foster care agency or case worker, make sure another mentor advocate is in the Cc line. Additionally, if you turn in a hard copy of any paperwork, make sure that you keep a copy in case you are asked to submit the same form again.

Once matched, a mentor within foster care must absolutely be predictable. You must show up, show up, show up exactly when, where and how you previously communicated. A foster care mentee usually expects disappointment. The agency worker will be reviewing your trustworthiness. Make sure you are known for your predictability and dependability.

You must also be known by your integrity, your ability to live out grace and truth. Children in the foster care system have experienced emotional trauma. Because life has been a game where the house seems to always win, you will be strategically observed long before you are trusted. You may actually perceive that your mentee does not like you, is annoyed to spend time with you or would rather be anywhere but where the two of you are together. This is an act. The mentee may have even convinced himself that it is true, but his soul is thirsting for a caring adult. Someone to encourage her, someone she doesn't want to disappoint. A mentor can be a constant thread in a confusing life story, but a mentee will be scared to hope for a very long time.

A major national study published in *Pediatrics* found that a child in foster care matched with a caring adult mentor for at least two years was more likely to report better physical health and less likely to report suicidal thoughts, acquire sexually transmitted diseases or engage in violence.[7]

If you are willing to take on the extra challenges and effort involved in mentoring a child in foster care, you can have a massive impact in that child's life. A mentor in foster care makes a difference. You can make a difference.

---

7 Study from Pediatrics, Official Journal of the American Academy of Pediatrics, http://www.pediatricsdigest.mobi/content/121/2/e246.full

13

Mentoring within a Literacy Program Chapter Thirteen

Mentoring is about relationship.

Some of the greatest by-products of this relationship are character development and skills transfer. Literacy is a game-changing skill for finishing school and gaining employment. There is a direct, inverse relationship between literacy and delinquent behavior – the more literate a young person is, the less likely he or she is to engage in delinquent behavior. A major national study which focused on adults with low literary rates concluded that more than 70% of Americans who read at or below a fourth grade level will spend a portion of their adult life in a correctional facility.

The lack of literacy in many urban schools is shocking. Teachers are under resourced and overwhelmed and do not have further capacity to help lead mentoring programs. Without a community or church supporting an urban school, many students pass through without critical literacy skill development and fall short of what they could become.

Literacy is a gift that many impoverished or at-risk children do not have. Many children have illiterate parents and are just following in their parents' footsteps. When a parent has not finished high school, it is more probable that the children will not finish. When a child cannot read, he cannot learn or have a bigger vision than what he sees. But reading opens up a world of knowledge. Descartes once said, "The reading of good books is like conversation with the finest men of past centuries."

Literacy also opens up opportunity. A child who cannot read is 100% dependent on others to fill out a job or college application, report the news, or engage in advanced thought. When children learn to read, they can navigate their own way – they can take life and career steps that illiterate children cannot. In the words of Dr. Seuss, "The more you read, the more you know. The more you learn, the more places you'll go!"

At The Mentoring Project, we see many wonderful organizations pair adults with children in one-on-one literacy tutoring relationships. It is critical for children to have literate adults invested in their quest to acquire this important skill. The Mentoring Project mentor training offers a foundation, a relational base from which you may build your literacy training. In this instance, a mentor community starts with The Mentoring Project training and then engages another step of intentional literacy training. This "layered" training creates a well-rounded mentor, one who is able to engage relationally as well as offer critical life skills such as literacy.

You can use your training from The Mentoring Project to expand your capacity as a mentor in a literacy-based program. A great deal of time spent with your mentee will be focused on the lesson at hand. This aspect of the program is very valuable because you are communicating, through your intense focus on your mentee's education, that you care very deeply about his or her intellectual development. This connection is very powerful. Your presence personalizes school and allows the mentee to safely express his comprehension or lack thereof. Where you see areas that need extra attention, you can provide focused help. When provided a safe environment to explore understanding, a mentee will engage more deeply in the lesson and have an increased chance of paying attention in class.

Depending on the format of the program, you will have some relational time each week with your mentee. Because a majority of your time will be focused on skill transfer, a relational mentor in a literacy program must listen and watch carefully for obvious and subtle communication from the mentee.

Is he more quiet and reserved today? Maybe he is experiencing something difficult outside of school. Is he hyper today? He may be excited about something good or anxious about something that seems overwhelming. Your job is to watch, listen and learn. What patterns do you notice with your mentee? How can you encourage him to work through frustration? What motivates him? Can you set up a scenario where he experiences the thrill of success?

14

Mentoring within the Urban Core Chapter Fourteen

If you did not grow up in the urban core, you will notice right away the differences between you and an inner-city child. He or she will have different values and a different perspective on life and will relate to peers and authority differently. If we do not understand our mentee's situation, we can inflict unintentional harm by assuming we share the same resources and ideals as our mentee.

For example, a mentor may think it is harmless to ask, "Why did you wear a t-shirt on such a cold day?" when the mentee may not have access to temperature protective clothing.

Or a mentor may wonder why a mentee does not wear clothes that "fit properly." The reason may not be based on style choice, but rather that the mentee only has access to clothing passed along by his older cousins. A mentee in the urban core may not experience control over his food choices and may struggle with weight not for lack of self-control, but for lack of healthy alternatives to fast or processed foods.

A mentee may not share the same health or safety concerns as his mentor. A young woman or young man may not necessarily assume that a pregnancy in high school is a "bad thing" – a pregnancy may be a status symbol, method of rebellion or a joyous chance to "get it right" for her baby.

It is critical for inner-city mentors to be sensitive and aware of these challenges. A child who does not value school may be prone to drop out.

The dropout rates of inner-city children often far exceed those of private or suburban schools.

Many inner-city children face trauma related to their home or neighborhood.

This trauma may be caused by one or both parents leaving the home, family members doing drugs or engaging in risky behaviors in the home, fearing gang violence or rape when she leaves her apartment, not having a clean and weather protected shelter and/or not having a steady address at all. We have heard several mentees tell stories of coming home from school only to find their entire "home" vacated and no signs of where their caretaker decided to set up their next place to "stay."

A child who faces trauma looks at the world very differently than someone who lives with food, shelter, clothing and in relative safety. Trauma may create a deep distrust of other people, especially authority figures and "caretakers." This trauma often turns a child "inward" and propels him towards numbing activities so much that he or she may genuinely not know how to communicate with or pay attention to adults.

The reality about mentoring inner-city youth is that the mentor may face a child with layers of trauma and negative expectations about the world, about others, and about life. The expectations may be far different from our own. For example, many inner-city children don't see education as a "way out." The government spends billions of dollars on education programs, but unless children (and parents) see education as valuable, educational programs may have minimal impact. First, children need to catch a vision about who they want to be, and who they are currently becoming, before they have the motivation to value education.

We believe the same principles work in the inner city that work in the suburbs and everywhere else. Mentors need to show up, to live out Christ, and to speak in – to coach with grace and truth. At the same time, mentoring in the inner city presents unique challenges and opportunities for the mentor. Here are some suggestions:

- Be extremely sensitive to the child's basic needs. Is she hungry? Cold? Is he going to school? What is happening at home? Listen. Try to understand everything you can about his or her situation.

- Use your differences as an advantage. Be yourself. Don't feel like you have to take on an "inner-city" persona or the verbiage. Don't be intimidated by your differences, but use them to introduce new experiences and behaviors. Talk about your background. Your life is a powerful model, and if a child is from an at-risk background, you may represent a totally different set of values. You may be the only college graduate they know. You may be the only person who has traveled out of state.

- After you have showed up faithfully, make sure to future-cast. This happens after you have been around awhile and have a place to "speak-in" to the child's life. Many children, and especially children from an impoverished or at-risk background, have had no serious thought about what they will do or who they will be in five years. They have no life plan. They have no ambitions or goals. Make sure you talk about the future, and then you can work backwards from there.

  Example: When a child decides he or she wants to graduate high school and pursue a college education, you can make a plan. What does it take to get there? What concrete steps do we need to take right now?

Many of these children have no idea or concept about the future or five years from now or maybe not even next week. If you ask them what they want to be when they are 18, their answers are simple or they give an uncertain shrug. One exercise we do is to have the kids write down what they want to be remembered for at the end of their life.

We ask: Who do you want to be, and what do you want to have accomplished? What do you want to be known for? Most kids do not know. This answer often takes a little bit or a lot of digging. These questions are a good lead in for a family conversation or even a faith conversation.

And if you're still having trouble getting started, sometimes it helps kids clarify what they do want by first seeing what they don't want. (i.e. I don't want to be in prison. I don't want to die early.) It's okay to give kids time to think about this. Your patience and encouragement might get them thinking about options they may have never considered for themselves.

ONGOING RESOURCES FOR YOUR MENTORING JOURNEY

PART FOUR

15

The Mentoring Project: What We Do Chapter Fifteen

The Mentoring Project exists to rewrite the fatherless story through mentoring.

We recruit, train and encourage mentors to show up for at-risk and fatherless children so they can have a better future. We believe in the transformational power of one-on-one mentoring. The Mentoring Project's primary function is to recruit and train mentors and connect them with matching organizations. Since 2009, some 4000 people have been through our mentor training, and many of these people have gone on to be matched in a mentoring relationship or engaged in a "natural" mentoring relationship.

Our mentor training materials are designed to equip mentors for their mentoring journey. These resources are available at REWRITE Mentor Training events, which are held live around the country and presented by TMProject staff.

The TMProject Mentor Toolkit is a great option for churches and organizations who aren't able to attend a REWRITE Mentor Training event. The TMProject Mentor Toolkit, available at thementoringproject.org/store, provides the materials needed to launch a sustainable mentoring community. The same mentoring principles shared at REWRITE Mentor Training are presented via videos and Mentor Field Guides. Also included is an Operations Manual with clearly outlined steps to hold a TMProject training and start a mentoring community.

The TMProject Mentor Toolkit is offered in two collections – individual and small group. The individual Mentor Toolkit includes training materials designed for the mentor focused on making a difference in his community. The small group Mentor Toolkit includes expanded resources for the leader of an organization or small group. The books, training videos and promotional materials in TMProject's Mentor Toolkit give leaders everything they need to launch or expand a mentoring effort in their community. And TMProject staff is always available to answer questions and help you get started.

After the training is complete and a mentor/mentee match has been made, we continue to encourage and resource mentors through our TMProject National Mentor Collective. We also provide unique activities for mentors and mentees called Mentor Moments. Both are described in more detail in the next chapter.

In addition, The Mentoring Project President, John Sowers, has been a strong advocate for mentoring and frequently speaks at conferences and events across the United States. By focusing on mentoring, we believe that the American church could effectively shut down prisons, end school dropouts, curb youth suicide, and reduce homelessness for a large number of youth affected by the fatherless epidemic.

16

The Mentoring Project: How You Can Join Us Chapter Sixteen

In the previous chapters we have set the tone for who we are, what we do, and why we exist. Now that you have a clear definition of what it means and looks like to be an effective mentor, we want to describe some of the benefits of interacting specifically with The Mentoring Project and ways in which to stay connected or contribute to our cause.

National Mentor Collective:

Individuals who attend our newly designed REWRITE Mentor Training events are invited to join The Mentoring Project's National Mentor Collective to receive powerful monthly resources to enhance their mentoring journey. In the past we have offered National Mentor Collective members several choices of books by favorite authors Tony Dungy and Bob Goff, and also from our founder Donald Miller. Another month, we supplied a specifically fashioned TMProject mug to further encourage mentoring. We try to present resources that are simultaneously fun, interesting and beneficial to the lives of mentors and mentees alike.

TMProject's National Mentor Collective members may be featured in The Mentoring Project's blog or other promotional campaigns. TMProject National Mentor Collective members will receive our monthly newsletter as well as other communications specially designed to continue equipping mentors to mentor their mentees and advocate for mentoring in their community.

TMProject National Mentor Collective members also receive exclusive invitations to TMProject Mentor Moment events that are sponsored by The Mentoring Project or TMProject affiliates. TMProject National Mentor Collective members have been invited to go backstage at Carrie Underwood concerts and meet the band before enjoying a VIP concert package. In the past, National Mentor Collective members were flown to the White House to meet the President and First Lady, complements of The Mentoring Project.

Advocate, Share & Contribute: We understand it is not feasible for everyone to commit to mentoring long term, but if you are holding this book in your hands, we have a pretty good idea you would like to be involved in this cause in some manner. Good news - you can advocate creatively! Several TMProject advocates have chosen to participate in rewriting the story of fatherlessness through a variety of creative approaches. Some have chosen to financially support TMProject by donating royalties from book sales, board game sales and ticket sales. Others have ridden across the country to speak about the mission of The Mentoring Project.

Here are some other ways you can advocate for, share and contribute to our mission:

- Pray for churches that are involved and those that will get involved. Pray for the children, mentors and guardians of xthe children who will be forever changed by mentoring relationships.
- Social media has become a brilliant tool for us to stay connected with our friends and followers. Become a fan of The Mentoring Project on Facebook (/tmproject.org) and share the mission of TMProject with your friends. You can also follow us on Twitter (@tmproject) and Instagram (@ tmproject) to interact and share stories, pictures and updates

about how TMProject is rewriting the fatherless story. Our annual "Don't Buy the Tie" campaign for Father's Day has been enhanced by a social media element, which allows our followers' pictures to be featured on the website, www.dontbuythetie.com.

- Volunteering with TMProject is a great way to engage with us relationally and serve with a mission. TMProject continues to grow, and we would love your help to keep up with all our activities. We host a number of events, many of which have been mentioned in this Mentor Field Guide. If you are hesitant about mentoring and/or still need questions answered, consider volunteering to learn more about our organization and ways in which you can personally make a difference.

- Give the gift of a mentor. Donors make it possible for The Mentoring Project to recruit, train and encourage mentors who are rewriting the fatherless story in their communities. We are grateful for those individuals who assist us financially so we can continue advocating and caring for the fatherless through mentoring. The Mentoring Project is primarily funded by donors who give $20, $50 and $100 a month. Online donations can be made at tmp.webconnex.com/tmproject. The Mentoring Project is a registered 501(c)(3) nonprofit organization, so your donation is fully tax-deductible. We are honored to partner with you in rewriting the story of fatherlessness.

17

Additional Mentor Resources
Chapter Seventeen

We hope you have enjoyed reading the material presented in the TMProject Mentor Field Guide. We cannot express enough how important these ideas are to us, and the fact that you have chosen to be a part of the story increases the significance. If you have questions about your mentor experience, please do not hesitate to contact The Mentoring Project. If you want to know more about mentor care, you may e-mail Kari, our Director of Strategic Initiatives, who oversees mentor care. Her e-mail is kari@thementoringproject.org.

If you are active online, please visit
www.thementoringproject.org for encouraging mentor updates.

Thank you for engaging your community through mentoring. Together we can rewrite the story of the fatherless generation.

THE MENTORING PROJECT'S

-FOR-

MENTORS & MENTEES

WWW.THEMENTORINGPROJECT.ORG

101: Activities For Mentors And Mentees

1. Have a picnic
2. Sign up to do a walk-a-thon or a 5K together
3. Create a music playlist
4. Go to the zoo, check for free admission days
5. Work on a puzzle together
6. Get an ice cream cone at a local ice cream shop
7. Visit a car show
8. Feed ducks at a pond
9. Play catch (baseball / football)
10. Visit a a farmer's market, enjoy fresh produce
11. Ride a bike on a local bike trail
12. Create a kite and try to fly it
13. Write letters to the troops
14. Visit an aquarium
15. Teach your mentee how to put gas in a car
16. Go to several garage sales and find old books
17. Create a mini book club, invite another mentor/mentee
18. Take cupcakes to someone on their birthday
19. Create an intro to archery
20. Help with science fair project
21. Decorate t-shirts with iron-on patches, paint, or buttons
22. Laser tag
23. Take a walking tour of a local college or university
24. Have a paper airplane building contest
25. Show your mentee how to deposit a check
26. Go for a hike
27. Ring the bell for Salvation Army
28. Attend a play
29. Shoot hoops; play a game of horse
30. Play chess
31. Indoor rock climbing
32. Volunteer to walk a pet
33. Tour a police or fire station

34. Create a holiday card for mentee's family or friends
35. Make a bucket list
36. Visit a botanical garden
37. Play tennis or practice your serve
38. Volunteer to rake neighbor's leaves
39. Attend a free festival or community event
40. Jump on a trampoline
41. Take your canvas to a park and paint a scene
42. Help with homework
43. Request a tour of a local radio station
44. Build a bonfire and roast marshmallows
45. Tie dye a t-shirt
46. Volunteer at an animal shelter
47. Visit a hardware store and dream up a project
48. Start a bug/butterfly collection
49. See a movie at a dollar theater
50. Complete a woodworking project together
51. Toss a Frisbee; invite friends to play Ultimate Frisbee
52. Thrift store shopping for school spirit days
53. Sell lemonade and donate the proceeds to a good cause
54. Create sidewalk chalk art
55. Feed birds at the park
56. Take your mentee through a drive-thru car wash
57. Play Hackie Sack
58. Have a watermelon seed spitting contest
59. Build a robot together
60. Attend a career day or conference at a school
61. Volunteer at a local soup kitchen
62. Make a quilt out of scrap cloth
63. Write letters to a community leader
64. Attend a free lecture at a book store
65. Put together model plane or car
66. Have a water balloon or snowball fight
67. Go grocery shopping and discuss healthy foods

68. Make a geocache or look for them around your town
69. Create a collage with pictures from old magazines
70. Watch street performers
71. Plant a tree or flowers
72. Attend a local sporting event (Jr. high, High school, Minor League or Pro)
73. Visit a new playground or park
74. Take pictures and get them developed
75. Attempt origami
76. Work together to check oil, tire pressure, wash the vehicle, etc.
77. Visit a planetarium
78. Play racquetball
79. Take your skateboard and visit a skate park
80. Play games at an arcade
81. Go to Hobby Lobby to look at craft kits
82. Volunteer at a local community garden
83. Paintball
84. Attend a local art exhibit; pick favorite and least favorite pieces
85. Make homemade ice cream
86. Rent a paddle boat or kayak
87. Play Apples to Apples or other engaging board games
88. Tour City Hall
89. Make a scrapbook
90. Go fishing
91. Write a short story together
92. Take mentee out for their favorite food
93. Create using Legos, K'Nex, or cardboard
94. Learn another language together
95. Get rolling at the skating or ice rink
96. Go to the library, find information on mentee's hero
97. Do a scavenger hunt
98. Visit a museum, check for free admission days
99. Go to an orchard and pick fruit
100. Make up a secret handshake
101. Learn how to juggle

The Mentoring Project's Mentor Collective allows mentors to receive monthly resources to help them along their mentoring journey.

FREE MENTOR RESOURCES

EACH MONTH JUST FOR BEING AWESOME?

Along with free resources each month, Mentor Collective members are invited to events and elite opportunities offered by TMProject andTMProject's friends.

JOIN THE MENTORING PROJECT'S

MENTOR COLLECTIVE

BY SIGNING UP ONLINE HERE

TMP.WEBCONNEX.COM/MENTORCOLLECTIVE

OR SCAN WITH YOUR MOBILE DEVICE.

Don't worry- we know we are super legit!

★ ★ ★

The Mentoring Project offers unique Mentor Moment events as the cornerstone of its mentor care program. Mentor Moments are designed to give mentors and their mentees a fantastic experience that, likely, neither the mentor nor mentee would have the opportunity to experience otherwise.

Past Mentor Moments have included backstage access on Carrie Underwood's Blown Away tour, meeting the President and First Lady, digging for dinosaur fossils and wild scavenger hunts across a botanical garden (just to name a few!).

-VISIT OUR BLOG ONLINE AT-

WWW.THEMENTORINGPROJECT.ORG

READ MORE ABOUT OUR MENTOR MOMENTS AND THE ROCK STAR MENTORS WHO SHOW UP IN KIDS' LIVES. THEIR STORIES ARE MOVING.

Training Notes

Training Notes

Training Notes

Training Notes

Training Notes

Training Notes

Training Notes

Training Notes

Training Notes

Training Notes